Photography is an exciting and versatile pastime. Whether you have a digital or manual camera, you can take photos to inform, amuse and even trick others with your pictures.

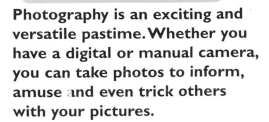

Give the Boot to Point and Shoot

Do you think of photography as the simple process of pointing the camera at the subject and shooting? The photograph a trustworthy record? Not anymore! Point and shoot is still possible, BUT anyone can do that!

Fun Photography

It is time to produce photographs that make people stop and look. How many people do you know that can SAFELY take a picture of somebody holding a head under their arm – or at least appearing to?

Camera Capers

Read on and you could be that clever photographer… Have your models climbing gigantic walls, losing their head or juggling several items all at once!

Cameras have only been around for less than 200 years, but they have progressed enormously in that time.

Mirror Images

Many years before photography was invented, a man called Charles de la Roche (1729–1774) wrote an imaginary tale called *Giphantie*. In this story, mirror images of actual images were secured on a canvas that had been coated with a special surface.

Invention

The invention of the process of photography was first announced to the public in 1839 but the specific date that photography was actually invented is unknown.

French photographer, Louis Jacques Mandé Daguerre.

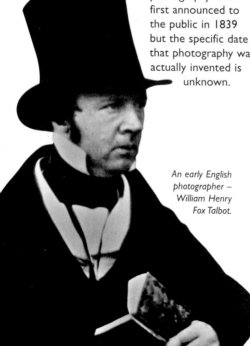

An early English photographer – William Henry Fox Talbot.

Anglo-French Ideas

The invention of photography was first announced in both England and France. In England it was revealed by a man called William Henry Fox Talbot and in France by Louis Jacques Mandé Daguerre.

Camera Obscura

There are two main scientific processes involved in photography. The first one is camera obscura, an aid, involving a prism, which enables artists to draw accurate replicas of the outlines of objects. The second process involves using materials which are permanently altered when exposed to light.

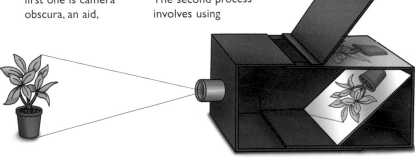

An example of a camera obscura. The image is reflected through the lens, upside down onto a mirror. The mirror then projects the image the right way up.

Niépce's heliograph – a view from his own window at Le Gras.

Negative

The first negative ever to be produced, in 1835, was very different to those we are familiar with today. It was not made out of a tough piece of plastic but of small, poor quality paper.

Exposure

The first successful picture made using materials that react to light was produced by Joseph Nicéphore Niépce in the summer of 1827. The exposure time was eight hours!

Manual cameras all have the same basic components: a lens, flash, viewfinder, back release button, rewind button and exposure counter.

Your Camera
Look at the diagram to find out where the basic components are located on your camera. For ease of use, virtually all of the operating buttons are located at the top of the camera.

Lens   Flash

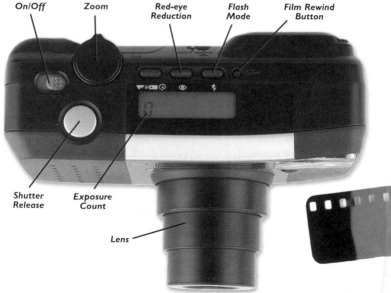

On/Off   Zoom   Red-eye   Flash   Film Rewind
                      Reduction   Mode   Button

Shutter   Exposure
Release   Count

Lens

Viewfinder

Back
Release
Button

Film Window

Film

All manual cameras require a film which, once the photographs have been taken, has to be processed. The film is coated with light-sensitive chemicals which, when exposed to light, reproduce the image you see through the lens.

Number of Exposures

Film Type

Film Speed

35mm

S.H.R.200

Lightproof Case

The film should only be exposed to controlled light from the camera's lens, so when not in the camera, it should be kept in its lightproof case.

The components on the camera all have a different function. Take a little time getting to know the way they all work as this will help you to get the best results from your camera.

Shutter Release

Exposure Counter
The exposure counter is a very helpful, if simple, tool. It lets you know how many shots you have left on your film.

Exposure Counter

Lens

Flash
The camera is equipped with a flashlight for when there is not enough natural light for a good picture to be taken. As the flash creates a brief, but intense, period of light, the picture is shot.

Flash

Shutter Release
This lets light into the lens in a controlled way.

8

Viewfinder
This is the view through the lens; look through this to compose your picture.

Rewind Button
You will need to rewind your film back into its light-proof case before removing it from the camera. This button allows you to perform this function.

Back Release Button
This will release and open the back of the camera where the film is loaded. Never open this before you have rewound your film, or you will ruin your pictures!

Flash Indicator
The flash indicator simply indicates if the flash is on or off.

Viewfinder

Rewind Button

Flash Indicator

Back Release Button

Read on for a little technical info on how your camera actually works!

Shutter

To take a picture you press the shutter release button. The shutter opens and closes to let a controlled amount of light into the camera.

Light

The light enters the camera through the lens. The lens is a curved piece of glass. Its job is to focus the beams of light that bounce off an object, into a real image. Within the lens there is an adjustable hole, or aperture. Together with the shutter, this controls the amount of light that is let into the camera. The amount of light required depends on the lighting conditions; in most cameras this is controlled automatically.

Chemical Reaction

This image is recorded onto film in the camera. Camera film is coated with light-sensitive chemicals. When exposed to the light of the image, these chemicals react and a picture begins to emerge.

The lens focuses the beams of light that bounce off an object.

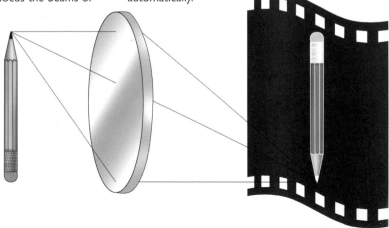

In a dark room, formulated chemicals react with the light-sensitive coating on the paper to develop the image.

Dark Room

The exposition of the film takes place in a dark room. There is no natural light in the dark room so the processor can control the depth of exposure.

Digital Development

One of the reasons digital photography is becoming so popular is that you do not need to develop your film. That's because digital cameras don't use film.

Digital photographs need no film which means that you don't have to wait for the photographs to be developed.

A manual camera needs to be fitted with a film which, of course, must be loaded correctly.

Processing

Processing the film produces a negative of the real image. A finished photograph is a positive image. When you take your film to be processed you will get positive prints and the negative film, which can be used again to produce further prints if you want them.

Film Types

There are different types of film available for use in manual cameras. Colour or black and white films are the main choices. However, you can get different speed film – fast speed or slow speed. Generally, fast speed film is used in dim light whilst slow film is used in a brighter light.

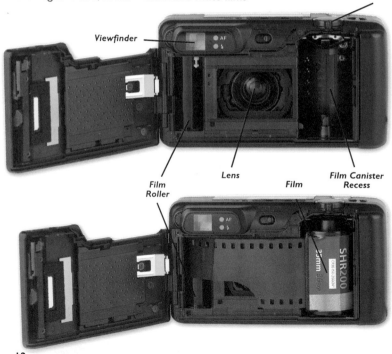

Viewfinder

Zoom

Lens

Film Roller

Film

Film Canister Recess

Loading...
Film is very simple to load; in the picture you can see 35 mm being loaded but in some cameras, the film is loaded slightly differently.

1. Place the film canister in the recess, as shown.

2. Push the canister in so it clicks and is secure.

3. Locate the film roller.

4. Pull a small amount of film from the canister and lay it across the film roller.

5. Close the back of the camera and the film will wind into position automatically. You are now ready to take a picture.

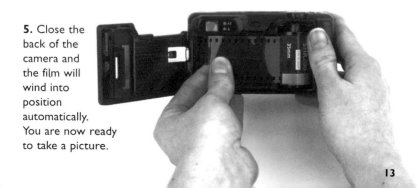

The digital camera functions in a similar way to the manual camera except that it does not use film.

How It Works
The main difference between a manual and a digital camera is that images are not recorded onto film, but instead captured by a matrix of light-sensitive cells and then converted into a digital format. The images are stored in a special memory module in the camera, called a flash card.

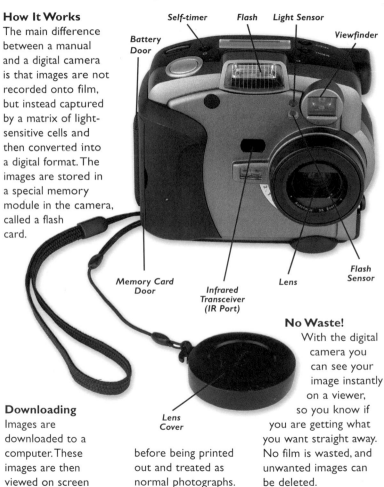

Self-timer · Flash · Light Sensor · Viewfinder · Battery Door · Memory Card Door · Infrared Transceiver (IR Port) · Lens · Flash Sensor · Lens Cover

Downloading
Images are downloaded to a computer. These images are then viewed on screen before being printed out and treated as normal photographs.

No Waste!
With the digital camera you can see your image instantly on a viewer, so you know if you are getting what you want straight away. No film is wasted, and unwanted images can be deleted.

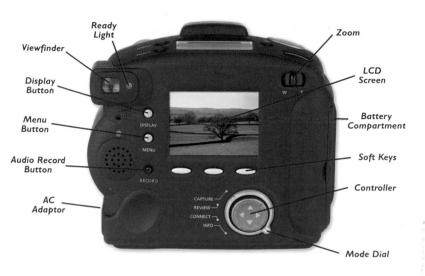

Viewfinder
Ready Light
Display Button
Menu Button
Audio Record Button
AC Adaptor

Zoom
LCD Screen
Battery Compartment
Soft Keys
Controller
Mode Dial

Uploading Your Images

When you have taken your photos, plug your camera into the computer with a USB cable. This is usually done via the keyboard.

Transfer

A camera icon will pop up on your computer desktop. Double click this icon to open up a window showing thumbnail previews. Select the

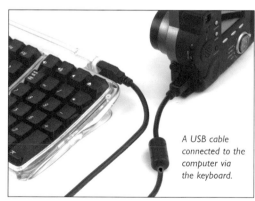

A USB cable connected to the computer via the keyboard.

pictures you wish to upload and drag them to the folder where

you wish to keep them. They will then be saved in this folder.

A camera, whether manual or digital, is an expensive piece of equipment. It is extremely important that you take good care of it. A good camera will last for years if maintained and looked after well.

A digital camera – the lens cap should always be replaced after use to protect the lens from damage.

A battery charger is vital for keeping a set of fully charged batteries ready for use.

Lens Cap

To avoid scratching your lens, always put your lens cap on and keep the camera in its case.

Battery Charging
Digital cameras use a lot of power, and need high-performance rechargeable batteries. Don't forget to take out your rechargeable batteries after each use and put them on charge for your next shoot.

Case
Always keep your camera in a camera case to protect it from dust, sand, heat and general damage.

Look after your camera by keeping it in its case.

Leaky Batteries
Don't leave run-down old batteries in your cameras, digital or manual, as they may leak and cause it damage.

Temperature
Make sure that your camera is not stored anywhere too hot, cold or damp. All these conditions will affect both the camera and the film.

Replacing the batteries in a manual camera.

Cleaning
Use a very soft cloth to gently clean away any smudges on the lens.

It's important to look after the lens and wipe off any smudges.

To make the most of your digital images, and even manually produced photographs, there are several other pieces of equipment you may need.

Personal Computer
Both Macs and PCs have programs which you can use to manipulate your digital photographs. For example, you may wish to change the colour of your subject's eyes.

You'll need a computer with a manipulation program for your digital photographs.

Digital Manipulation Program
There are a few computer programs that you can use – *Photoshop* elements, *Paintshop Pro*, *Corel Draw* and various simple programs that may come with scanners.

A flatbed scanner.

Scanner

If you do not have a digital camera, you can scan in normal photographic prints and even pictures from magazines. The scanner creates a digital image, which can then be manipulated.

Colour Printer

If you would like your digital photographs on paper and not just on screen, they can be printed at home if you have a colour printer. These days, however,

Print out your pictures at home with a colour printer.

Canon's IXUS V3 and printer.

you can connect your digital camera to a specially made photo printer, without the need for a PC.

Photo Quality Paper

Use photo quality paper to give prints a professional photo finish.

19

Other Equipment

Tripod
This will help to keep the camera still while you are taking photographs and composing your shot.

Capture some favourite moments of your pets and friends.

Subjects
Friends, family and pets are essential as models for your photographs.

By following the rules even the most impressive photography will appear easy but remember, even professionals can make mistakes. Use this simple guide to keep your pictures looking good.

Prevent Obstruction

Do not take a photograph with unwanted items, such as fingers, hair or the camera strap, in front of the lens.

An obstruction over the lens has ruined this photograph.

Blurring, caused by not keeping the camera still.

Prevent Blur

Do not move the camera whilst taking a photograph, especially in low-lit conditions.

Prevent Total Darkness

Do not take a photograph without first removing the lens cap.

21

Out of Focus

If you are too close to or too far away from your subject then your picture will be out of focus.

An out of focus shot – too far away.

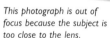

This photograph is out of focus because the subject is too close to the lens.

Bleaching

Bleaching is the term used to describe a picture that comes out too bright. To avoid this, do not point your camera directly towards the light source.

Bleaching is caused by facing directly into the sunlight.

Cutting off Part of the Subject

Never take a photograph without ensuring that the entire subject is included.

Under-exposure

To avoid under-exposure, do not take a photograph without a flash in poorly lit conditions.

Left: Heads cut off and bodies sliced in two by not aligning the subject within the frame.

Below: An under-exposed photograph.

Sometimes what seem like 'mistakes' can actually produce clever results if executed with thought.

Dizzy effect.

Blurring

Move the camera or the subject to evoke the sense of movement. The photograph on the right could illustrate how the world looked through the eyes of someone feeling dizzy.

Deliberate Bleaching

Take the photograph directly towards the source of light if you want to lose the identity of the subject. The photograph on the left could be used in a murder story where you wish to keep the suspect's identity a mystery.

By aiming the camera lens at the light, you lose the detail in the foreground of the picture.

Obstruction
Take a photograph
with a shape
directly in front
of the lens. The
photograph here
was taken with a
shaped frame cut
out of card held
by the model.

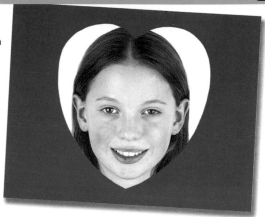

*You can create any
shaped frame in order
to achieve this effect.*

You can produce some interesting photos by simply changing the angle at which you hold the camera whilst taking the picture.

Portrait
Hold your camera vertically, perpendicular (at right angles) to the ground.

A portrait photograph.

A landscape photograph.

Landscape
Hold the camera horizontally, parallel to the ground. Your picture will be wider from left to right, but shorter from top to bottom.

Going, going, gone!

Diagonally

To produce a really wacky photo, hold the camera at a 45-degree angle to the ground.

Movement

To take a picture showing movement, focus upon one point so that only the edges look blurred.

Blurred edges of a moving subject.

If your camera has a 'zoom' facility you will be able to either move in close or move out from your subject to produce some really interesting photographs.

Zoom In

By getting very close to your subject, you may see details that you do not normally notice. A lens referred to as a macro lens will produce the best results for this. Alternatively chose part of an item (anything that you have in your house

A close-up view of a flower showing a good deal of detail.

or garden, it need not be unusual) to photograph and you could produce a guessing game.

Use a zoom lens to get really close to your subject.

Can you guess what object was photographed here? The answer is at the side of the page.

Zoom Out

The greater the distance between you and your subject, the more you will be able to capture within a single image.

Right: A zoomed-in image, but what is it?

Below: A zoomed-out image of a hillside.

Answer: A whisk

The camera never lies is a well-known phrase but, with a few simple tricks, you can make it seem as though it does!

Fooltography!!

To make it appear that your model has taken their own head off you will need two assistants. One will need to sit on a wall with their back to the camera and drop their head so that it is not visible to the camera. The second person will need to face the camera with only their head visible above the wall.

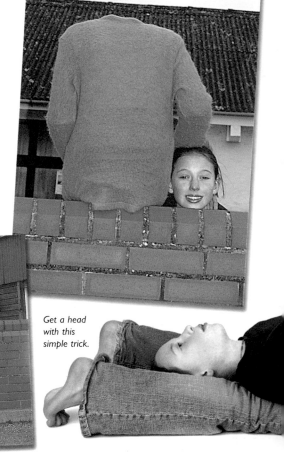

Get a head with this simple trick.

Impossible?
To make it appear that you have very flexible friends you will, again, require two people. One needs to lie on the floor on their front facing the camera. The second will need to lie on their back, on top of the first person but with their feet facing the camera. Make sure that only the legs of the person on top actually show in the picture.

That looks painful — but how is it done?

This is how it's done.

From Outer Space!

This photographic evidence shows that UFOs really exist! Spray a frisbee and a small plastic bowl with silver paint before allowing them to dry completely. Fix the bowl onto the frisbee using a strong glue or double-sided tape and throw it into the air, making sure that no-one is standing in the way!

A homemade UFO.

Take a photograph of the frisbee against a plain sky to make it look as though you have captured a UFO on camera.

An unidentified flying object!

Heads Off!

This trick looks as though your friend is holding someone else's head under their arm. To do this, stand a smaller person behind your friend with their head hooked through the other friend's arm. Make sure the body of the smaller person is hidden from view by the friend.

This is how it's done.

You must take the photograph from the correct angle or you'll give the game away.

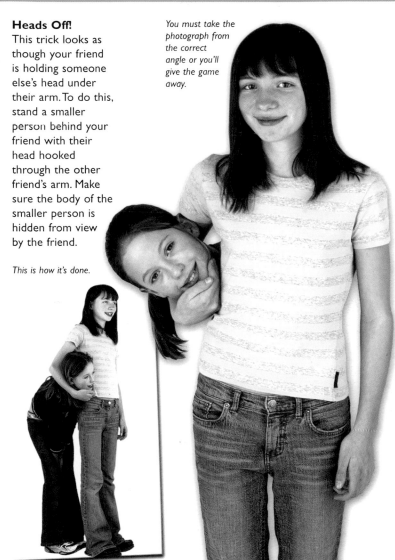

The digital photograph can be changed and manipulated to show whatever you want.

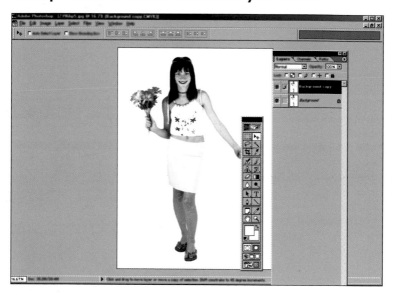

Selecting

To select part of a photo to copy or manipulate, create a path with a pen tool, this can then be turned into a selection; or use the lasso tool to create a selection directly. You may find Copy and Paste under the Edit menu in the top bar of your program.

Move
The Move tool may be found at the top right hand corner of the Tool Box.

Layers
If your program has layers, you can put each element of your montage on its own layer. This will help you to edit. Select a layer by clicking on the layer icon with your mouse. Move the layer by selecting the move tool, and dragging the layer into position with your mouse or keyboard arrow keys.

Changing Size
To change the size of an image you will have to change its size on it's whole layer. Select the layer and use the scale command, which may be found under Edit > Transform from the top bar.

Opacity
Turn into a spooky ghost, by double clicking on the layer

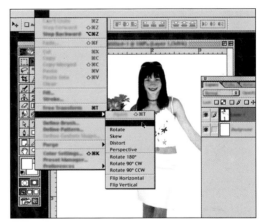

icon you want to fade, and then experimenting with the opacity slider.

Don't forget that if you don't have a digital camera, normal photographic prints can be scanned into your computer and made into digital images.

Here are some more great tricks for you to try.

Well Travelled

To make it seem like you've been to China you'll need a picture of yourself in front of a plain background and a picture of the famous landmark. Use your Picture Editing program to open the picture of yourself.

• Draw a path around the figure that you wish to use. Copy the image inside the boundary that you have created.

• Open your background image. You can paste your figure onto the background as a separate layer.

• Move the figure around until it is in the correct position.

• You may also need to change the size of the figure to fit in with your background.

Create the illusion that you're actually standing on the Great Wall of China.

Prop up Pisa

If you want to be more ambitious then forget about standing on the Great Wall of China, and try propping up Italy's Leaning Tower of Pisa instead. The principle's exactly the same and your friends are sure to enjoy the joke.

Such strength! Create the illusion of yourself propping up the Leaning Tower of Pisa.

My Pet's a Monster!

By making the image of yourself very small you can make it seem as though your cat wants to eat you!

Cat-astrophe! You can also shrink yourself to the size of a mouse to become a hungry cat's dinner!

37

Superhero

To become a superhero simply cut out the head from one of your pictures before pasting it onto the body of your favourite character.

UFO Sighting

For a digitally created version of the UFO trick, simply cut out a picture of a UFO then paste it onto another digital photo.

Special Effects

You should be able to put an outer glow around your UFO, depending on the program that you are using.

Above: Transform yourself into a superhero by combining a picture of yourself and your favourite character.

Below: A digitally created version of the UFO trick.

Be a Supermodel

You can change the colour of your clothes and even your pets!

To do this, the figure, the clothes, and the dog need to be on their own separate layers. To change the colour of a layer you can use one of the Image Adjustment tools. Hue/Saturation is probably the easiest to use, this is found under Image > Adjust under the top menu bar. Move the Hue sliding bar until the

Fancy a change?

colour changes. Experiment with these controls until you achieve your desired effect. If you want to, you can save several versions of the picture in different colours – depending on what your mood is!

Using the desired settings, you can create new colour images!

Do you trust your eyes? Seeing is believing, isn't it? Not necessarily – these camera tricks will fool the unsuspecting onlooker.

Distance
To make something appear very small, place it in the distance. Have another object in the foreground to use as a comparative frame of reference.

Right: This girl looks as though she is picking up the tree because it is further away than she is.

Below: The illustration shows how it's done.

Foreground

To make something appear very large, place the object in the foreground, close to the camera.

Above: The illustration shows the girl standing well away from the shoe to give the appearance of her standing inside the shoe.

Left: This boy looks as though he is standing inside the boot.

Below: This clever trick is very easy to set up.

How to achieve the wall-climbing trick.

Climbing the Walls

To make it appear as if your model has amazingly climbed a huge wall, get them to crawl along a brick driveway.

Juggling Act

This clever trick photography makes it appear as though your model is expertly juggling several items. Ask your model to lie on the floor with the items arranged in an arc above their heads.

Then take the photo from above. This could either be taken from the vantage point of a balcony, from standing on a step just above the subject or by simply standing over the model.

Main picture: The model and the items are not actually in an upright position even though it appears that way!

Far left: How it's done.

Pushing up the Wall

To make it appear that one of your models is holding up a large object such as a wall or building, take the photograph from an alternative angle. A plain background such as the sky will assist in the creation of this illusion.

Above: A clever camera trick that alters perception.

Left: Great strength is needed to hold up this wall – or is it?.

Have fun experimenting with all sorts of optical illusions involving your camera and the art of false perspective.

If you are not content with your static photos and want to put some life into them, why not try some simple animation?

Stills

An animation is made up of many separate still images, each slightly different to the one before. These images are seamlessly put together, and made into a moving picture.

Digital Animation

The digital camera can make this very simple, as most have an animation function. Instructions for this will come with your camera.

Manual Animation

If your camera does not have an animation function, why not make a flicker book? Animations do not have to be long, but you will need a lot of photos. To produce a flicker book you will need to write a script for your animation before taking a sequence of photographs to illustrate each step.

Step by Step

Make sure that each photograph only shows a slight change in one part of the image. For example, move just one arm at a time. To make your images even more convincing you could show one action being carried out over several stages – this takes a lot of patience and you will need many photographs to complete a short animation.

Flicker Book

Flicker books are a series of pictures that alter slightly, tricking the eye by giving the impression of movement. To make one you will need to cut out all the stills and stick them onto small pieces of card all the same size. Stack the cards in order so that the sequence of stills runs from front to back of the stacked cards. Secure the cards with an elastic band and, holding firmly in one hand at the end with the elastic band, use your other hand to flick the book. You will notice that the series of stills seem to show movement just as a film playing frame by frame.

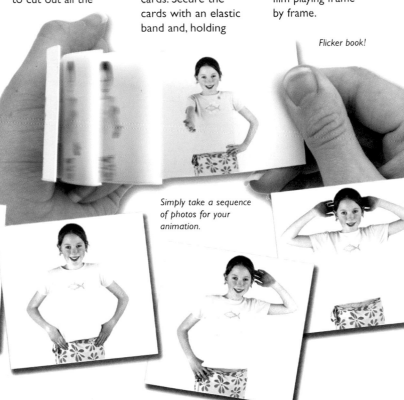

Flicker book!

Simply take a sequence of photos for your animation.

Confused by any terms used in this book?
Check their meanings here.

Animation
A method of producing the illusion of movement from a presentation of successive images.

Aperture
A system of metal leaves which open and close to create a gap controlling the amount of light falling onto the film.

Automatic focusing
Automatic focusing is a device on most modern cameras, which sights your subject and automatically brings it into focus.

Back release button
This will release and open the back of the camera where the film is loaded.

Camera obscura
A device involving a prism which projects a 3D image onto a flat surface.

Digital image
A digital image comprises pixels or points of light, each with its own colour, stored in a computer file.

Digital image manipulation program
A piece of software which allows you to edit and manipulate digital images.

Exposure
The combination of time and intensity of light needed by the camera to create a good negative. The shutter and aperture control this light.

Exposure counter
This tells you the number of photographs you have already taken so you know how many shots you have left on your film.

Film
A strip of plastic with a light-sensitive coating designed to run through a camera.

Film cassette
This light-tight/trapped metal or plastic container for a length of light-sensitive film enables the film to be loaded into a camera in full light.

Glossary

Flash
An artificial light source that is used to help gain correct exposure when lighting conditions are poor.

Focus
The positioning of the lens to ensure a clear image. Most cameras are built with an automatic focus setting.

Lens
A transparent material, curved on both sides, through which the photographer views the subject.

Lens cap
A plastic protective cover to help avoid damage to the lens.

Light source
The light falling on the subject, whether it is artificial, natural or a combination of both.

Negative
An image on film in which the light and transparent areas represent the dark tones and the dark areas represent the light tones of your original subject.

Perspective
Perspective is the representation of a 3D object on a 2D surface.

Photomontage
Making an image by cutting out and pasting together several separate photographs.

Processing
Processing the film produces a negative of the real image.

Rewind button
Rewinds the film back into its lightproof case before it is removed from the camera.

Scanner
An electromechanical device, that scans the printed image, which is then loaded into your digital image manipulation program.

Shutter
The shutter opens and closes to let a controlled amount of light into the camera.

Stills
An animation is made up of many separate still images, each slightly different to the one before.

Subject
The person, or object, being photographed.

Tripod
The stand used to keep the camera steady.

Zoom lens
A lens designed to zoom in (close up) and zoom out (long shot) from the subject.

Shutter speed
Controls the amount of time light is allowed to shine on the film.

Viewfinder
Look through this to compose your photograph.

Zooming in
Getting very close to your subject so you can see details that you may not normally notice.

Zooming out
Using the zoom lens to allow a greater distance between you and your subject to capture more within the one image.

Photography credits:
Cover: (tl) Comstock; (ml) Canon (UK) Ltd; (br) Photodisc. 3: (bm) Action Press (ACT)/Rex Features. 4: Getty Images. 5: (m) Getty Images. 19: (bl) Canon (UK) Ltd. 24: Kate R. Kydd. 29: (t) Kate R. Kydd.